THE
Family
BOARD MEETING

You Have 18 Summers
to Create Lasting Connection
with Your Children

OUR PURPOSE IS TO STRENGTHEN FAMILIES

We believe there is nothing more important than the relationships we create in our life, especially those with our children. When we strengthen these relationships, we automatically live a happier, more fulfilling life.

Our team is committed to providing our community with simple rhythms, lessons and experiences that harness the power of quality time, deepen connection, teach the important lessons not taught in school and create moments that will last forever.

The starting point is our *Board Meeting Strategy*, explained in the pages within.

INTERNATIONAL ACCLAIM

for *The Family Board Meeting*

After our first Board Meeting, Jack looked at me and asked, "Dad, when can we do this again?"

DAVID BACH, Nine-Time *New York Times* Best Selling Author

Spending 1-1 time is such a "simple" concept in theory, but the nuances make the difference.

YANIK SILVER, Author, Evolved Enterprise

F-ing brilliant! Gamechanger.

STEVE SIMS, Owner, BlueFish

There's been a massive increase in trust between me and my son, and we've adopted a number of family-first practices as a result.

GARY PINKERTON, Navy Submarine Commander

I've been doing Board Meetings with my daughters since meeting Jim in 2013. They're so valuable, it's ridiculous.

JAMES ALTUCHER, *New York Times* Best Selling Author

For my gorgeous girl and our four spirited children: Alden, Leland, Magnolia and Sampson—you are my inspiration.

CONTENTS

FOREWORD

By Hal Elrod,
author of *The Miracle Morning*

I n the fall of 2016, I was diagnosed with a very rare, aggressive, and often fatal form of cancer—acute lymphoblastic leukemia.

The diagnosis, of course, was a shock; the odds, even more so. I was given a 30 percent chance of survival—and that would be after a difficult course of treatment that would leave me weakened and vulnerable.

It's at times like these when priorities have a way of making themselves abundantly clear. While I never once entertained the idea that I would succumb to my diagnosis, a parent with a life-threatening illness can't help but feel overwhelmed, uncertain, and, of course, afraid.

My biggest fear was dying and leaving my children without a father. I also knew that my children would face many of the same fears and emotional struggles that I would during my treatment and recovery.

Fortunately, we had something to turn to.

The previous year, I had met Jim Sheils at an event where we instantly connected over our shared, deep desire to be the best dads we can be. I had already heard of Family Board Meetings, and at the event, I met about a dozen other dads who had implemented the practice with their families. Each, in their own words, emphatically expressed that the process had improved their relationships with their children more than anything else they had ever done.

I left the event with Jim's book, a slim, engaging read aptly titled *The Family Board Meeting*. I read the book on my return flight home to my family and was even more convinced. Right away, I implemented Family Board Meetings with my daughter, Sophie (8), and my son, Halsten (5). My wife and I could immediately see how much our time together meant to them.

After my diagnosis, our Family Board Meetings took on a whole new level of meaning. While our family was forced to deal with the myriad of emotions that accompanied my illness and treatment, our consistent Family Board Meetings allowed us to stay connected, create new memories, and most importantly, talk openly about how we were feeling.

The meetings are wonderfully unique to each child. Sophie prefers daddy-daughter experiences centered around getting dressed up and going out on nice dates, while Halsten loves to do something fun, like go to the park or play laser tag and arcade. So far, with each Family Board Meeting we have, the experiences, conversations, and memories we've shared continue to deepen our connections and enhance our communication.

Even at the best of times, these crucial conversations with our children are often lost in the shuffle of busy day-to-day life. At the toughest times, these connections can vanish altogether. Family Board Meetings ensure that the quality time to connect—which we and our children crave—is never missed.

With the cancer fully in remission and life returning to normal, we're still having our Family Board Meetings. When Jim asked me to write the Foreword to the new edition of *The Family Board Meeting*, I jumped at the chance because I practice it and I truly believe it is one of the best practices that a family can adopt.

To me, just being good enough is simply not good enough—especially when it comes to being a parent. I believe we owe it to our children to become the best version of ourselves so that we can be the exceptional parents that they deserve.

I hope you, too, will immediately implement Family Board Meetings in your family's life, because I know you and your kids will be all the better for it. There's no better gift you can give your kids than the gift of yourself and your undivided attention.

With love,
–Hal Elrod

BEFORE WE BEGIN

_____

(A short note about the new edition)

A lot has happened since the first edition of _The Family Board Meeting_ came out in 2015.

The book began as a way to help change what I saw as one of the most tragic challenges of modern life: the disconnection of busy entrepreneurs from their families. I was saddened to watch these talented, wonderful people drift away from their children on a tide of distraction, stress, and regret.

It wasn't long, however, before the book's message began to spread. The entrepreneurs that we worked with started to share the philosophy—first with their key employees and team members, then with friends and family members, who passed it on in turn. Slowly, but surely, our little book for helping entrepreneurs built into a growing wave that rolled out from the business community to the world at large. So much so that we had to create an online community of family support. If you'd like to be a part of this community, we'd love to share with you and hear from you. Visit us at www.facebook.com/boardmeetingstribe.

Since then we've been overwhelmed—and overjoyed—by the stories of success that have rolled in from around the globe. I am often greeted at events with, "Oh! You're the family guy!" and I couldn't be happier to hear those words used to describe me. To know that one simple idea—an idea born on the waves and then spread through families in a ripple of connection—has had such an impact, is one of the great joys of my life.

I've also been delighted to discover how our simple process for reconnecting parents and their children doesn't just work for busy entrepreneurs but works for *everyone*. From teachers to doctors, carpenters to chefs; we now know that the Family Board Meetings process works for anyone, anywhere in any type of work or family situation.

In hindsight, of course, it makes sense. After all, it isn't just entrepreneurs who want and need to connect with their children. It's *everyone*. In this time of distraction and often overwhelming demands, who *doesn't* want that? Connection, it turns out, is universal.

This edition of *The Family Board Meeting* does two things to help make that goal of connection even simpler to accomplish. First, it expands the language and application of the original book to make it accessible for everyone. No matter what work you do, or how busy you are, the three simple steps in the pages that follow can, without a doubt, transform your relationship with your children.

Second, we've added an FAQ section to help people deal with the most common pitfalls and uncertainties along the way. If there's a snag in your Family Board Meeting, chances are you can untangle it in the pages that follow.

Although we call these important meetings *Board Meetings*, I have heard others call it Daddy Day or 1:1 or Date Day. No matter what you call your time together, the principles are still the same.

As you begin to read, know this: *it is always possible, and never too late, to connect deeply with your children.* This is true regardless of your age, your work, or your circumstances. I believe that in the pages ahead, you'll discover that *The Family Board Meeting* isn't just a tool for entrepreneurs to reconnect with their kids; it's a rhythm for changing lives.

I hope the rhythm moves you.

–Jim Sheils
   Spring, 2018

INTRODUCTION

Someday Never Comes

Almost a decade before this book was born, I left the house one morning for what I would come to think of as my "slap in the face."

Life, for me, was going well. I'd built a successful real estate investment business and along the way had the privilege of spending time with some extraordinary mentors. We'd take what we euphemistically called "Board Meetings"—surf trips where we worked on personal and business development but also spent a lot of time on the ocean doing what we loved.

I'd learned an incredible amount from those retreats. I was able to watch as accomplished business people deftly balanced the enormous demands on their time and energy with the even more important demands of raising families and maintaining the bonds of friendship. It was inspirational, and it was educational; I was truly fortunate.

From those early board meetings, I'd begun to help other entrepreneurs—a practice that developed into informal retreats, and then a full-fledged program of helping parents reconnect with their children, against the backdrop of ocean-based activities like surfing. I loved the work, I loved the results, and I loved making a difference.

What I was about to see that day was the other side of the equation.

That morning, I accompanied a good friend to a detox clinic—an important step in his battle with alcoholism. As part of the program, each addict had to bring one friend or family member to the clinic for support; my friend had chosen me. With us were five other addicts, each accompanied by a loved one. I was, however, the only friend in the support group—everyone else had brought a parent.

As we settled in and got to know one another, people began to gradually open up. With the support of trained counselors, our discussion deepened.

At some point, I sat upright. Something was up. It was as if a red flag was waving in my mind. *There's something important here,* I thought.

Then it hit me: as the stories unfolded, I realized that all five parents in the room were successful entrepreneurs. At first, I dismissed it as coincidence, but then I reflected that my friend's parents were *also* entrepreneurs. That was the red flag, waving in my mind: for every busy, business-owning parent in the room, there was also an addict.

My head began to spin as I made the connection. How could this be? I loved being an entrepreneur, and I didn't want this to happen in my family. Were my kids at risk? Were my entrepreneurial friends at risk? Were their kids?

Just as quickly, though, I realized that business wasn't the root of the problem. After all, I'd seen many incredibly successful entrepreneurs who were deeply connected to their children.

So what was the common thread?

Memories came flooding back. My friend's parents were good, hardworking people who had raised three children. Yet, the older kids hadn't faced the same challenges—only my friend, the youngest of the three. Why? Unfortunately, their business was struggling at the time when my friend needed them most. As they put in extra hours at the office to save their business, my friend was the only sibling left without the one thing that makes the difference in every child's life: *quality time.*

During our discussions, it became increasingly clear that it was the lack of this vital element that was to blame, not entrepreneurship. None of these hardworking parents had spent quality time with their children during the formative years. They had invested heavily in their businesses, but not in their kids. The result was predictable. There was a lack of connection, which led to confused teens, who in turn made bad choices. Those bad choices then followed the teens into adulthood. Now, those confused teens were confused—and addicted—adults.

As I struggled to understand how this could happen, it became apparent that many of the parents there that day had once believed the great lie of success-seekers everywhere: that they were "doing it for their kids" and that their kids would, someday, understand.

Someday never came.

Instead, those busy parents experienced the pain of watching their children morph into something unrecognizable as alcohol and drugs tightened their grip.

That day, I watched "successful" grown men and women sobbing at the clear knowledge they hadn't been there for their children when it was most important. It was enough to change me forever. That day, I learned there was something more important than money, more important than fancy private schools, and more important than empty gifts. That something is called quality time.

I sat in that room, listening to the devastating stories and the heart-wrenching regret of each parent, as a hundred different threads wound themselves together in my mind. The disconnected entrepreneurs and corporate warriors I'd met over the years. The disconnected parents in the support group. The memory of my friend's disconnected upbringing. It was like a slap in the face—an abrupt shock that left me wondering, *what happened to these families?*

When I look back, I know that it was in that moment that this book was born. The moment when I realized that I was seeing more than troubled kids or busy lives; I was witnessing the fallout of a disconnection epidemic.

I walked away that day knowing I had to help find a solution.

—1—

THE MOST IMPORTANT QUESTION IN THE WORLD

There was a time when it was mainly busy business owners who brought their work home with them. In a world of structured, predictable work days, a large chunk of the middle class could leave the office at the end of the day and leave work behind, too. You could say goodbye to your job, at least for the night, and join your family for dinner. You could spend unfettered weekends together.

That's all changed.

Now, it doesn't matter if you're a freelancer, a business owner, or an entry-level employee in a large company. It doesn't matter if you're a plumber, a coder, or a manager.

The story for everyone, everywhere, is the same: we *never* leave work behind.

How did this happen?

Harmlessly, at first. We wanted to get ahead, so we worked a little harder. We got caught up in making progress, making payments, making hay. Then screens and devices came along, and that meant we could make *more* progress. *More* payments. *More* hay.

Or, that's how it seemed.

Ironically, along the way we forgot one of the fundamental reasons we were working so hard: we wanted to support our families—especially our kids—and we wanted to develop the freedom to spend quality time with our family on our own terms.

What we failed to notice was that the efforts we made to financially support our children were undermining our ability to emotionally support them. The devices that seemed to so effortlessly connect us were, in fact, dividing us.

We, all of us, were slowly, inexorably, drifting apart.

We were—we *are*—disconnecting.

THE MISSING TIME

Of course, we still "spend time" together.

Right now, for instance, you may be thinking, "Come on, Jim, I take my kids to baseball, piano, and gymnastics. We eat dinner together at the table, and we watch TV together after homework is done. We spend lots of time together."

Those parenting activities are wonderful, and I commend you if you do them. They are part of a successful parent-child relationship. But while spending time with kids is important, time alone will never result in a true connection between parent and child because true connection requires something more than just time.

To understand that missing piece, let's use your workplace as an analogy. Imagine if you just showed up at work and spent the whole day doing...well, *nothing*. Just drinking coffee, watching videos, eating lunch, maybe going out for a drive. You'd have spent a whole day "with" your work, but accomplished almost nothing. You'd have put in the *time*, but it was empty time—time without intention or focus.

We have expressions for this in the professional world—we call it "face time" or "putting in time" or "logging hours." They're all ways of describing *time without quality*, and we all know the kind of results we get from simply putting in time.

Sadly, however, those phrases also describe how we often spend time in our personal lives. We're logging hours and putting in time, but it isn't the kind of time that connects us to our kids, creates intimacy, and forges strong bonds. It isn't *quality* time.

Quality time is something different. It's time with purpose. Time with focused attention. Time where we shift our focus away from ourselves and our worries and place it, with intention, on someone else.

Quality time is what's missing in our family lives, and it's what our kids need the most.

WHY WE DON'T SPEND MORE QUALITY TIME WITH OUR KIDS

We intuitively know this. Ask anyone you meet, and you'll find the same result that I do when I speak to people in workshops around the world: *the vast majority of people admit they don't spend enough quality time with their family, especially their children.*

But why? After all, almost everyone would agree that their children are their top priority. Why don't we put in more of that essential ingredient of quality time?

To be clear, it isn't for lack of good intention. We all have great plans to spend quality time with family. But consider this: if you relied only on good intentions to do your job or build your business each day, how would you be doing? Probably not so well. Succeeding in your home life, like your professional life, requires more than just intention—it requires execution. And that means *intending* to spend quality time with your kids isn't the same as actually *doing* it.

What's stopping us?

Part of the reason we aren't giving our kids the quality time they need is that *we think we already are.* Yes, there are those parents who simply don't spend *any* time with their children, but I've found it's far more common for parents to put in low-quality time and mistake it for something else.

Much of this is due to changes in the world of work. You may, for example, be thinking any of the following:

- "Thanks to technology, I have more flexibility than ever. I can be with my kids during work hours."

- "I make my own hours. I can spend time with my kids whenever I want."
- "I work from home. I see my kids all the time."

But just like driving your kids around and watching TV together isn't quality time, working with your kids nearby isn't quality time either.

At the heart of all of these stories is a single truth: *we don't understand the difference between time and quality time.*

- Yes, your phone might enable you to keep tabs on work while you play hooky for the afternoon and stay home with the kids, but *that time is not the same as quality time.*
- Yes, your success might buy a better vacation and a nicer school and a beautiful home, but *those things are not quality time.*
- Yes, the logistics of getting kids to and from school and sports and clubs and friends and camps means you are together. *But that time is not the same as quality time.*

There is no replacement for quality time. Not your success. Not the trust fund you create. Not your hard work, or the gifts you buy, or the neighborhood you live in. What your kids need is true connection, and to achieve this, you need not just time, but quality time.

Remember: *time together isn't the same as quality time together.*

THE QUESTION

Here's a simple way to know if you've been spending quality time with your kids. Simply answer this question:

When was the last time you spent a whole day alone with your child, with no electronic distractions, while enjoying a fun activity and meaningful conversation?

It sounds simple, but if you're like most busy parents, you will answer that you can't remember a single time.

Yes, you read that right—*a single time.*

I've seen world-beating executives and tough-as-nails contractors tear up over that one little question on our retreat questionnaire.

They get emotional because reading this question is the moment they first understand the difference between time and quality time. And it's the moment they realize they've been depriving their kids, and themselves, of the one thing they need most. At that moment, they realize that, in spite of their best efforts, they don't have the answers. It's the moment they begin to grasp the consequences that quality time impoverishment is creating.

It's also the moment when they are confronted with a deeper question—the most important one they'll ever have to answer:

What is more important, your work or your children?

⁊

11

JENI'S STORY

"Our oldest, Hoyt, who is just shy of four years old, has been experiencing night terrors for a couple years now. There have been nights where Hoyt went through a night terror for hours where he isn't in a full state of consciousness, and it is truly terrifying for him and us as parents. Even more, at daycare, Hoyt has been showing some bullying signs and having difficulty listening. The week prior to Jim's presentation, our daycare lady told me, 'he was in and out of time out for an hour.' It was so hard to hear that as a mom.

After Jim came to speak with us, that night I sat down with Hoyt and asked him what was something he liked to do with just daddy and then just with mommy. He told me he likes riding the lawn mower with dad and going to the park with mom. So that night, pressed with time before bed, we tried a mini Board Meeting. For an hour he and I went outside and played. Then he and dad rode the lawn mower together. I know this isn't exact Jim's method but I was curious. Before bed, he was talking up a storm about how much fun he had.

The next day, when I picked up Hoyt, both daycare providers told me separately, it was like Hoyt was a different kid; he didn't have any time outs and was playing so well with the other kids.

Fast forward a couple weeks, still very few time outs at daycare and at home.

Jim's presentation made me realize, as he puts it, there is a difference between time together and quality time together. We do many activities as a family but never realized the important impact doing activities one-on-one with each of our kids could have. Hoyt is the first-born grandchild on both sides and therefore has a very special bond with all of his grandparents. He is often going to the farm with my parents or fishing with my father-in-law on weekends but does not have a lot of time with Mom and Dad without little brother. We have now made it our goal to balance this quality time and already can see huge strides of improvement and success with him."

❦

CONNECT WITH OUR COMMUNITY

Readers of *The Family Board Meeting*, along with those already implementing the strategy, have created a community of like-minded parents from around the world to support each other in this journey. This is a strong online community in which to connect, support, share best practices, learn from one another and discuss the book. Check it out here: www.facebook.com/boardmeetingstribe.

THE QUALITY TIME
REVOLUTION

So that's the bad news: we're disconnected from our kids, and we've been fooling ourselves about it.

Here's the good news: I've seen the solution to this disconnection problem in action.

Over the years, I've learned from some amazing mentors who were excelling professionally, but also knocking it out of the park as parents by regularly spending quality time with their children. They're the living *opposite* of the disconnection problem.

On one of the original board meeting surf trips with these mentors, I sat staring in disbelief as an eleven-year-old boy spoke to his dad openly, honestly, and with enormous respect. It was as if I was watching an advanced civilization; there was just something different, something *incredible*, about the way my mentor Craig and his son Russ interacted with each other.

At the time, I grasped that it had something to do with the time they spent together, but I knew a lot of other dads spent time with their kids without achieving the same effect.

What I was witnessing, of course, was the impact of quality time.

I suspect you've caught glimpses of this, too. Perhaps you spend time with your child but, if you're like most parents, the time is standard parent-child stuff. You're hurrying them out the door, correcting behavior, and giving them instructions (or *orders* if you're more of the drill-sergeant type).

But, occasionally, aren't there moments of magic? Times when you and your child are on the same page and having fun, and you experience a fleeting moment of togetherness? It's in those moments that you remember what matters most. Things just feel right and you're overcome with an incredible feeling that puts a positive spin on everything. That feeling is called *connection*, and it's created by quality time.

And we need a lot more of it.

We need more quality time so we can eliminate disconnection. We need more quality time so we can create powerful and lasting change in our relationships with our children.

What we need is a quality time revolution.

THE BOARD MEETINGS STRATEGY

I'm sure you know the feeling of truly connecting. I'm sure you've felt those moments of magic. But do you know how to create that feeling consistently? Through my mentors, and then through work with hundreds of parents around the world, I learned that not only is quality time important, but *you can create it deliberately and predictably,* with just a few simple steps.

We call those simple steps the Board Meetings strategy, and it will help you get below the surface relationships with your children to a true connection. Not only that, it will also keep you accountable and consistent, so you keep improving your relationship with your kids. The Board Meetings strategy will even ensure you can answer yes to the tough questions that run through your mind:

- Am I getting through to my child?
- Does my child appreciate what they have?
- Would they make the right decision if I weren't watching?
- Would they come to me for advice before their friends or the Internet?

Every parent wants these results, and the Board Meetings strategy is perfectly designed to deliver them. Better still, it's already been tested and proven by hundreds of families around the world.

The parents using this strategy consistently report incredible results. They talk of finding a new joy in parenting. They talk of reconnecting. And, in what I find most moving, they talk of profound changes in the lives of their children, who begin to transform before their eyes.

There are many great stories, but I can't think of a better way to illustrate the power of the Board Meetings strategy than by sharing one from my own life.

ALDEN'S STORY

We were already several years into the Board Meetings strategy development process when I had the opportunity to use it in my own life.

My chance arrived when I fell in love with Jamie, the woman who would become my wife. When I won her heart, I also got a chance to win the hearts of two beautiful boys; Jamie was divorced with full custody of Alden and his younger brother, Leland.

The boys and I hit it off right away (and I've since adopted them), but I still had my work cut out for me. Both boys, rightfully, had trust issues from difficult life experiences that happened before I met them.

Alden, the older of the two, was especially troubled.

When I met Alden, he'd just been placed on the autism spectrum at school, where he was a very challenging student on the brink of failing. Those were difficult obstacles and we wanted solutions to them, but far worse, he also suffered from night terrors.

Consider yourself lucky if you don't know what night terrors are. The condition usually affects children, who wake up in the night in a half-conscious state, screaming in abject terror. It often takes two or three hours to shake them out of their disorientation and get them back to sleep. It's upsetting for everyone but especially for the child, who experiences enormous fear.

I knew that Alden's trust issues were at the root of his problems, and I wanted to reassure him that he'd never need to worry about those problems again. I knew that if he could understand he was safe and consequently regain trust for the adults in his life, he'd get better.

But how do you explain that to a kid? I wanted to just tell him, but I knew that kids respond to our actions more than our words. Saying the words too soon, or in the wrong context, wouldn't work like I wanted them to. He had to *feel* trust, not just hear about it.

This is why we always tell parents that the very act of going on a Board Meeting is the most powerful thing they can do for their relationships with their kids; words can never convey what time and consistency can.

Not long after Jamie and I got together, I began having Board Meetings with Alden and Leland.

I followed the exact process discussed in this book, and I can pinpoint the moment Alden began trusting me—the exact moment which set off a chain reaction of change within him.

True change takes place during special moments of connection because breakthroughs happen when we're open, trusting, and connected. This was exactly what happened with Alden.

The moment occurred at the end of a Board Meeting. We'd just had a fun day together, and by giving him my whole attention without interruption, he saw my commitment, which started to build trust. In that state of true connection, I simply told Alden that he'd never have to worry about the problems he'd had before.

That's when a beautiful thing happened.

I saw a shift in his eyes. It was a small shift, but it was a start, and from that day on, as we continually made deposits to our relationship, Alden began to change, day by day. Jamie and I both spent a lot of time with him, but as we maximized quality time, we saw steady improvement as our connection deepened and he trusted more.

Every parent knows when their child goes through a positive change. We don't need external evidence to prove this; we *know* it. In Alden's case, however, we happened to have external benchmarks—his autism diagnosis, his falling grades, his extreme night terrors.

Within one year of applying the Board Meetings strategy, we saw stunning changes. Jamie and I began to notice shifts in every aspect of his personal life. He was more relaxed, carefree, creative, and confident. He participated more in sports and friendships. He got along better with his brother.

At school, his transformation was remarkable. From near failure in his grades, Alden went on to make the honor roll and was awarded the most improved student for the entire third grade. In an extremely rare move, the school psychologist even retracted the autism diagnosis, admitting it to be a mistake.

We were extremely proud of his improvements at school, but they were a small deal compared to the biggest change of all: to everyone's enormous relief, the night terrors had stopped.

What had changed to make all of this happen? Just the implementation of Board Meetings. There was no medication, no therapy. What Alden needed was focused and fun quality time that would make him feel appreciated and safe.

THE REVOLUTION IS IN YOUR HANDS

I don't think I'd recognize the old Alden if I saw him now. Today, he's a strong, capable, intelligent, and athletic young man. He's a voracious reader and is already helping me with my real estate business. He's well-liked, well adjusted, and one of my heroes. When something needs to be assembled, fixed, or altered around the house, Mom and Leland go to Alden for help before me!

Throughout all my years of entrepreneurship, all the parents I've helped and taught, and all the investors I've created wealth for, nothing has been as rewarding as helping Alden feel better. Nothing. I would have given my entire real estate portfolio for the results we achieved with Alden, but I didn't have to, and neither do you.

If you think this story is amazing—and it is more amazing than I can portray—then I urge you to take action and create your own remarkable story. Your child might not have the same challenges Alden had, but regular Board Meetings can and will improve their life. I know this because every person on Earth needs true connection, and quality time is the way to achieve this.

Stories like Alden's—and there are many of them— are more than just good news stories. They're a blueprint for taking back quality time. They are tales of revolution.

What's more, *they're not difficult.*

This revolution is something that we all have the power to participate in. It doesn't take much time, it's extraordinarily fun, and it practically ensures that you'll leave a legacy of connection to your children, and they to theirs. If Alden's story inspires you even a fraction as much as it inspires me, then I know you'll want to learn, understand, and implement the Board Meetings strategy.

The last thing I want, however, is for you to be inspired without a clear plan to implement this process in your own life. The following sections of the book will explain exactly why and how this life-changing strategy works. In the pages ahead, I'll share the proven (and fun) three-step process that harnesses the power of quality time and is simple enough to integrate into your busy life right away.

Welcome to the quality time revolution. To go beyond inspiration and into execution, please read on.

—3—

THE BOARD MEETINGS
STRATEGY

When you think of a traditional board meeting, the first image that probably comes to mind is a boring, 1980's-style IBM conference room, where a bunch of stuffed suits sit around a table crunching numbers and talking to each other like robots.

Fortunately, things have changed. There's a new world of work, and its spirit is catching on. Board meetings are occurring in more exciting places, often with fun activities involved.

If you ask company leaders why they use this new style of board meeting, they'll say it shows appreciation and unites the team.

I couldn't agree more.

The purpose of a board meeting is to track results, reconnect the team, and to prepare them for the next ninety days. Not everyone has board meetings, of course, but most of us understand the importance of meeting with our biggest investors, clients or colleagues on a regular basis.

The secret sauce of the best professional meetings is to make them a consistent, focused, in-person discussion. I've personally experienced the power of this. By staying engaged with our top investors, I've raised millions of dollars for our real estate company. The consistency of these meetings deepens the trust I have with my investors, many of whom have become genuine friends. This experience has taught me that in business, nothing can replace face-to-face meetings. The price of the occasional airline ticket to discuss an issue with someone is worth it, as being in direct contact is far more effective than a Skype or conference call will ever be.

HOW THE BOARD MEETINGS STRATEGY WORKS

For Family Board Meetings, we take the best parts of effective, consistent, focused, face-to-face meetings and use them to connect with your children. It's a proven way to maximize quality time, and it's the whole point of the Board Meetings strategy. We must treat our kids with the same level of respect that we do our work colleagues and business associates.

The process is as simple as it is powerful. Here's how it works: once a quarter, you will have a Board Meeting with your child. It must be a minimum of four uninterrupted hours. After that, there are only three steps to success during your time together.

You must:

1. Be one-on-one with your child
2. Have no electronics
3. Do a fun activity of the child's choosing, followed by focused reflection

The result of this mix of elements is a perfect combo—just like a peanut butter and jelly sandwich. And just like the sandwich, you'll only see partial results if you only use part of the formula.

MEETINGS THAT ACTUALLY WORK!

If there's one thing almost all of us have experienced, however, it's a bad meeting. How many times have you sat in a room and thought, *This is pointless—why am I even here?* Meetings have a bad rap, and for good reason. Many of them *are* pointless.

These meetings are different. They're different because the objective is clear—a deeper connection with your children through quality time—and the process itself is built on very specific principles that ensure that *the meeting does what it's supposed to do.*

Imagine that.

But, don't just blindly take my word for it. I want you to understand why the strategy works. Studies show that when we understand why something works, we're far more likely to integrate the practice into our lives.

The next chapter of this book is dedicated to teaching you why Board Meetings work by showing you the principles that make the strategy a consistently powerful way of deepening your connection with your children.

༄

ZANDER'S STORY

"Our Family Board Meeting story began when I read an early version of Jim's book back in 2013. Soon after, we started our "date days."

Jim's idea was simple: what if you dedicated a day to all the key relationships within your family? Business owners and executives do this for their business, but few do it with their key family relationships.

Our kids were 4 and 7 when we started, so there was no resistance to the idea. They quickly fell in love with the Family Board Meeting days. The kids always talked about them and planned for the next one.

We followed Jim's protocol, focusing on decompression. We didn't put pressure on having breakthrough conversations, just allowing space for whatever might come up.

But the most powerful board meeting moment happened with my son about 18 months ago. We had a fun, decompressing day followed by a great meal. But it was during the drive home that he brought up the topic of puberty.

This surprised me. He was only 9 years old at the time, but I soon learned about his experience. Not knowing what to expect, he was surprised to notice bodily changes and different feelings. He thought these changes would be obvious to everyone else and that he'd be judged.

When I got home, I Googled the normal age ranges for children to begin puberty. Sure enough, 9 is about the youngest that boys will begin the process. I was a late developer and don't remember experiencing any symptoms until I was at least 13, so this was all very new to me.

Over the years, my son and I had plenty of Family Board Meetings together. So we had a strong rapport. I'm convinced that this is why he was comfortable discussing puberty with me. Together, we discussed his fears. I reassured him that everything he felt was normal. At the end of the board meeting we both felt incredible. It was a feeling of fulfillment very different from regular markers of success. It was one of my proudest moments.

In his book, Jim promised that kids will treat you as a confidante after holding proper Board Meetings. He said they'd come to you, instead of friends or the Internet, when looking for solutions to difficult subjects. He was right!

Everyone should do this. It's the best way to connect with and support your kids."

−4−

WHY BOARD MEETINGS WORK

The Board Meetings strategy doesn't successfully connect you with your kids by accident. Like every successful process, it's driven by a series of proven principles—fundamentals that are true, regardless of family or situation.

This isn't new—you apply principles in your life every day, often without realizing it. If you're committed to health, for example, you eat well and exercise because those are proven principles for health and fitness. Follow them, and you get great outcomes.

Similarly, the Board Meetings strategy is based on a few well-proven fundamentals that ensure, as long as you follow the three steps, that you'll get the same great outcome every time—in this case, a better and more lasting connection between you and your children.

PRINCIPLE #1: SCHEDULING

There's a reason that we allow calendars to run our professional lives. Without them, important things get missed, forgotten, or bumped to that neverland of "someday." And we all know when someday comes.

Effective professionals know that the calendar is their secret weapon because *that which we schedule gets done.* It's that simple. It may seem silly to schedule a meeting with your child, but I challenge you to reconsider that. Could you imagine not scheduling appointments with the top clients in your business? Or not writing down and blocking off a scheduled meeting with your boss?

Absolutely not. Now, it's time to give our children the same respect.

Once a Board Meeting is scheduled with your son or daughter, then a big part of the job is already done. You'll be shocked to discover how effective this simple principle is in overcoming obstacles to quality time together.

There should never be a 90-day period when a Board Meeting isn't scheduled. At the end of each meeting, we recommend reviewing the following three months of your calendar and finding a four-hour block for the next. This ensures you build momentum from one Board Meeting to another.

If you don't schedule Board Meetings, they won't happen. Period. In fact, talking about a Board Meeting and then not doing it is even *worse* for relationships.

Promising quality time and then not following through hurts kids. You'd be better off not bringing up the idea in the first place.

Remember that consistency and follow-through are key. Don't let the simple task of putting something in your calendar ruin your opportunity to connect. It only takes a few moments. Make the scheduling ritual part of the Board Meetings process.

PRINCIPLE #2: REPETITION

The power of 90 days is one of the key principles of our Board Meetings strategy. By having a Board Meeting with each of your children every quarter, you begin to create a habit through the simple power of repetition.

Why 90 days? Performance experts use 90-day increments because it's a proven interval that is short enough to keep attention focused on an individual goal, yet long enough to evaluate progress.

In this case, your goal is to build a relationship and grow your connection with your child. For that job, 90 days is the perfect amount of time to maintain focus on the task and to evaluate progress from meeting to meeting.

PRINCIPLE #3: ANTICIPATION

Anticipating an event is always half the fun. Think back to what it's like to be a child at Christmas, your birthday, or an annual family vacation. If you were like most kids, I know you got excited about those events.

Research says that a proven path to creating happiness is to plan a vacation. Notice I didn't say *taking* the vacation; it's planning that's key. Planning the vacation contributes to happiness because anticipation is so pleasurable.

Anticipation works even better with a bit of time to build. Waiting 90 days is long enough to build anticipation without losing a child's attention. Kids disengage if they're separated from the event for too long, and you'll lose momentum in building your relationship if you wait longer than three months between Board Meetings. Remember, our goal is to maximize quality time, and part of that is creating the right amount of anticipation.

Likewise, having Board Meetings too often doesn't work, either. We don't want our children to take these experiences for granted, and if they happen too regularly, the experience becomes mundane. Just as a birthday would lose significance if it were every week, so does a Board Meeting if it's held too often. To maintain the mood of a very special time between parent and child, 90 days is the magic number.

PRINCIPLE #4: REFLECTION

The principle of reflection works in tandem with the principle of anticipation. Just as it's powerful to have something to look forward to, it's also powerful to have memories to look back on. Having a Board Meeting every 90 days is like having a pipeline of fresh memories and lessons to draw upon while building a relationship.

In our professional lives, we reflect on the successes of the past for inspiration, to learn lessons, and to craft a strategy for going forward. It's important to reflect on previous Board Meetings for the same reasons. Reflection makes sure the lessons stick, the feeling is imprinted, and the anticipation builds. Again, 90 days is the perfect stretch of time to allow for powerful and ongoing reflection.

PRINCIPLE #5: DECOMPRESSION

What does it mean to decompress? The dictionary says decompression is "relieving pressure or compression." In other words, it means relaxing and unwinding. This is the entire point of having at least four hours of uninterrupted time for a Board Meeting.

Relationship building happens when people are decompressed. If you don't believe me, try to think of all those wonderful relationship-building moments you've had with your kids while on the phone, rushing them to and from school. There aren't any.

Most parents hurry their quality time with their children, fitting it in between a text and an email while hovering over the kitchen table for a quick breakfast. It doesn't work. Both the parent and the child need time to decompress.

Decompression doesn't happen immediately—in our work, four hours seems to be a magic interval. Any shorter, and you don't quite reach the level of relaxation you need to truly engage with your child. Any longer, and attention starts to wander, or people begin to avoid Board Meetings because the time commitment is harder to make.

By following the four-hour rule in your Board Meetings, you'll allow time for decompression and connection, while ensuring your meetings are enjoyable and realistic to schedule.

PRINCIPLE #6: MAGNIFICATION

Just as it's easier to see small details under a magnifying glass, it's also easier to see the intricacies of your relationship when you put intense focus on it.

The truth is always the best place to start, and the Board Meetings strategy allows you to see your relationship for what it really is. Just as you can't improve your finances or your fitness without first making an honest appraisal of the current reality, neither can you improve relationships without first seeing the problems.

Increasing the focused intensity of quality time also proves to your child that they are your top priority. This may seem obvious to you, but it won't be so obvious to them—especially if your actions don't support the idea. You can tell them a million times that they're a priority, but words will never prove it to them as well as a single, properly executed Board Meeting.

PRINCIPLE #7: SIMPLICITY

I've had more than one person tell me, "I can't believe this is so simple. Why didn't I think of it?"

One of the most magical aspects of Family Board Meetings is their simplicity. It's so easy to understand and so simple to put to work that it's almost difficult to *not* do. In a world where people are choking on content yet starving for execution, Family Board Meetings are a calm island of simplicity. Don't *worry* that the idea is simple; *relish* it.

⊗

Any great coach will tell you how important fundamentals are. It's these seven principles that operate behind the scenes, forming the foundation that ensures your Board Meetings deliver the joy of lasting connection with your child.

Now that you know the underlying principles, it's time to discuss the three steps to connection so you can get on with scheduling your own Board Meetings!

—5—

THE THREE STEPS

The Board Meetings strategy is so elegantly straight-forward that, based on the three simple steps I've already described, most people are able to put the strategy to use with their kids right away.

It's helpful, though, to have a deeper understanding of each step and why it's so important to follow all of them.

STEP 1: GET ONE-ON-ONE

As usual, the most elegant solution is the simplest. To deepen connection, *just get one-on-one*. The magnification and decompression principles simply don't take effect unless there is one-on-one time. This first step is vital.

One-on-one time has helped build wonderful parent-child relationships, saved marriages, and created world-champion sports teams. Therapists and personal development experts worldwide base their philosophies and practices on the power of one-on-one time. Almost universally, they find that communication opens up when two people are alone together.

Despite how well we know it works, however, one-on-one time is a sorely underused practice to develop deeper parent-child bonds. You might think the power of one-on-one time is painfully obvious, but this doesn't mean it's widely practiced. Many of the people we've spoken to could not remember a single moment of one-on-one time with their kids. Others could remember some moments, but most admitted they didn't have much one-on-one time. Very few had regular one-on-one time.

It's easy to fall into the trap of thinking that *any* time with your kids is true quality time. It isn't. When it comes to connection, any more than two is a crowd.

You might also think you're off the hook for one-on-one time because you only have one child. Not true. The same applies if you work from home. Even though both of those things may give you more time with your kids, that doesn't mean it's *quality* time.

This lesson was brought home by two attendees of our experiential education programs, in which all the parent-child pairs that attend learn how to surf together.

I will never forget Chaz and his mother, Ali. The memory of Ali stepping out of her comfort zone and riding waves while her son looked on with pride was an inspiration.

It was what Chaz said during his child interview that really struck home. We always ask kids about the quality time that they spent with their parents, giving them the definition of quality time and emphasizing the importance of it being one-on-one.

I'll never forget his answer. When Chaz heard the definition, he gave a puzzled look and said, "Well, my mom works from home, so we really don't get the chance to spend much quality time together."

As a busy entrepreneur with the flexibility to work from home, I can't begin to tell you how impactful this was on me. I was shaken to consider that there could be such a downside to what I felt was the perfect career.

Ali is a great mom and has a better relationship with Chaz than most parents do with their teens. However, Chaz gave us something that day that we all need to hear: *just because you work from home or have one child does not guarantee you're sharing quality time.*

Don't break the one-on-one rule. If you insist on bringing anyone else along, it's not a Board Meeting. Give your kids the gift of individual, focused time together. You'll be glad you did.

STEP 2: DISCONNECT TO RECONNECT (NO ELECTRONICS)

Inviting electronics along for a Board Meeting has the same effect as bringing along another person. There must be absolutely no electronics during a Board Meeting. Failing to follow this rule will sabotage decompression and the magnifying glass effect.

A few years ago, I had the pleasure of hearing bestselling author Dr. Ned Hallowell of Harvard Medical School speak at a private event. I was amazed by the authenticity and power of his message. My wife and I began reading his books and exploring his research on the phenomenon known as *screen sucking*. He explains the phenomenon like this:

> *"Held by a mysterious force, a person can sit long after the work has been done or the show he wanted to watch is over, absently glommed onto the screen, not especially enjoying what he is doing but not able to disconnect and turn off the machine."*

Sadly, most of us can relate to this empty feeling. Too much screen time is damaging to anyone. According to Dr. Hallowell, however, screen sucking is especially damaging to kids. He's done the research that proves the ill effects on mind, spirit, and relationships.

Like me, though, Dr. Hallowell is *not* anti-electronics—he's pro-connection. There are appropriate times for screens, but a Board Meeting isn't one of them. Board Meetings may be simple, but they are also delicate; one distraction from a text, a quick phone call, or an email will disrupt the focus.

Have you ever been reading an email or talking on the phone when your child is trying to talk to you or ask you a question? Do you remember giving them an incomplete or incoherent response? Guess what: your child noticed your attention was elsewhere. When you allow yourself to be distracted, your child feels cheated and less important.

Some of you will say, "Yes, but my calls and emails are important." I understand. So are mine. I'm not suggesting you stop taking phone calls or replying to your email. But do your children the service of not doing it during your Board Meeting.

The rule is simple: no texts, no emails, no calls, *no screens*. Your phone is off. No sounds, no alerts, no vibrations. Your computer is off. The TV is off, too—screen sucking together in front of a TV is no better than screen sucking alone.

I'm not saying a family show or movie is a bad thing. There are times and places for that. Just don't waste your valuable Board Meeting time on a screen. There are plenty of other things you can do with that precious time to strengthen your relationship.

The only exception is this: toward the middle or the end of a Board Meeting, it's a good idea to snap a photograph to commemorate the event. The photo can play an important role in the reflection process after the Board Meeting. If you're going to do this, switch your phone to airplane mode before the Board Meeting begins, or bring an actual camera. Do not allow screens to destroy your quality time.

I know dropping electronics is a big step for many. The first time you put this step into practice, it might feel awkward—you might feel anxious or stressed, as I did. Simply remind yourself that the world will not come to an end if you're disconnected for four hours while you reconnect with your child.

Once you get into the habit, you'll even find there's a freedom to turning off your phone. It feels great, and you'll likely start looking for more opportunities to do it. It wasn't until I started putting aside electronics for Board

Meetings that I finally established boundaries with the devices in my life.

My boys always know that my phone is off during our Board Meetings. We've even made turning my phone off into a ritual that we do at the beginning of each meeting. I'll say, "Okay, the phone is going off. Time for our Board Meeting." Or, I'll say, "Is my phone going to be on today?" They'll look at me with a smile and say, "Nope."

My young boys love it, and even teenagers will appreciate the commitment you're making, although they might give you a little hassle about having to turn off their own phones and personal devices. Don't give in. Stick to the rule.

Turn off the devices. Turn off the phones. Turn off the personal messengers. Turn off the computer. Give your Board Meeting and your child the time and energy they deserve.

STEP 3: CHOOSE FUN ACTIVITIES, WITH FOCUSED REFLECTION

I'm a huge fan of 1980's comedy films, and one of my favorites is *Ferris Bueller's Day Off*.

Without a doubt, the classroom scene with actor Ben Stein teaching economics helped to make this movie legendary. His monotone voice is unforgettable as he drones on to the students who sit bored out of their minds. I still remember laughing hysterically in my chair in the Madison Theater at the age of twelve.

The scene hits home because *it's true*. We've all had a teacher like that. We've all been in that classroom. We've all been put in a box and forced to "learn" while wanting to bite our own hands off because the lesson was so boring.

And yet, although we hated it ourselves, for some reason we try to use this same ineffective approach with our own kids. In a feeble attempt to strengthen our relationships, we lecture them instead of involving them. Whether we like it or not, we've all sounded exactly like the Ben Stein character at times. We've all put our children in uninspiring environments in an effort to get to know them better.

It just doesn't work.

By taking a different approach—fun activities with focused reflection—we get the environment working for us instead of against us, and the magnification principle really takes effect.

When you use this approach, you'll stop sounding like Ben Stein or Charlie Brown's teacher. Instead, you'll start connecting with your kids while having fun. Yes, it's true: *you* (but more importantly, your child) will actually have fun on a Board Meeting!

There's a common misconception that kids find adults boring; what they really find boring is interactions with adults that suck. Many kids have built up an aversion to adult company simply because most of the time, their experiences aren't fun.

What if, rather than forcing kids into a box where they don't want to be—which only creates *more* separation between parent and child—you let them choose something they love to do? What would happen if you just spent time with them in that space?

What happens is that they open up, and a new, deeper connection begins to flower. In a world that doesn't promote these types of experiences, we must choose them intentionally.

Here's how step three works: for every Board Meeting, your son or daughter selects a fun activity for the two of you to do together. It has to be something of *their* choice, not yours. The activity has to be something they want to do and that they're happy doing—not something that only you love.

If you like car shows but your child has no interest in them, you're not going to drag them to a car show for a few hours and consider that a Board Meeting, saying to yourself, "Wow, isn't it great that we bonded." This will only perpetuate disconnection. They get to choose the activity, and it doesn't have to be anything too fancy or expensive.

By letting your son or daughter choose the activity, they take immediate ownership of the Board Meeting. They feel like they're doing things on their terms, and this helps build a new layer of trust.

This is especially helpful for parents that don't have strong relationships with their teens. Disconnected teenagers may be reluctant (or flat out refuse) to do something together with their parents. Letting them choose the activity helps.

Letting them choose is also a great way to find out more about your son or daughter's interests, which can change quickly. One minute they're interested in children's movies, in another it's teenage pop stars. A day later, it could be pro football. Each Board Meeting gives you another window into their rapidly-changing life.

As the old saying goes, "Once you get someone laughing, you can tell them almost anything." By giving your kids the right to pick the activity, they buy into the concept. More importantly, decompression happens best when they get to do a fun activity of their choice. Having a relaxed, decompressed, and happy child makes the Board Meeting successful.

Share a fun activity together that your child chooses—you'll set the stage for focused reflection, and open the lines of true communication to establish a deeper relationship. That's where true magic happens.

THE POWER OF FOCUSED REFLECTION

The focused reflection period is where everything comes together. This is simply time at the end of your Board Meeting that's set aside to have open dialogue with your son or daughter.

By this time, the magnifying glass is fully focused. You've shared a fun activity together and probably had a meal. You're both decompressed, and it's time for you to really connect with your child.

Many parents get nervous about this part, but it's easier than you think. It can be as short as five minutes—in fact, we recommend keeping it short, especially when starting out.

Remember that just by going on the Board Meeting, *you've already won*—there's no pressure to say the right thing during focused reflection. In fact, there is a risk in saying too much, which can sabotage the trust built up during the Board Meeting. Just relax.

After spending several hours participating in a fun activity with your child, you've reached a point where you are both open to real connection. The last thing you should do at that moment is run through a list of fifty lectures you've been meaning to give your child. The focused reflection isn't a heavy lecture time. You have already said plenty simply by being there. The key is not to fixate on or worry about the conversation you'll have. You want open communication to happen naturally during the focused reflection, with no pressure.

The idea of this last part is to develop a lesson or discussion from the activity you experienced together. The more developed and practiced you are at this, the more you can tailor your lesson to the experience, but when you're just starting out the best icebreaker is to ask this simple question:

What was your favorite part of today?

Many, many parents have used this question with great success on their Board Meetings, and it's remarkably effective in helping kids open up in unexpected ways. Your child may surprise you with what they open up about after you ask that question. Many parents (especially of teenagers) have told me the conversation during focused reflection often goes way off course into deeper subjects the parents never thought their teenager would bring up—things like sex, drugs, and peer pressure. It can be shocking at first, but that's the power of true connection.

If kids start to share these serious topics, the best way to support them is to just listen, or give an example of when you were similarly challenged at their age. Don't try to be a superhero. Let them know that you had challenges, that you were afraid, that you had friends who made you feel unwanted, or that you had issues at home. Tell the truth. They'll feel more relaxed and look at you more as a person and less as an overbearing parent when you do.

Be prepared, however, that there's a reasonable chance your child may not open up immediately, especially during the first few Board Meetings. It can take time to build trust, and a heavy expectation about opening up can undo the fragile early stages of your connection. Just be there for them, create consistency and trust, and ask them that simple question, "What was your favorite part of the day?"

☙

There are plenty of opportunities for adults to develop on their own, and equally as many chances for children to develop on their own, too. Sadly, there is far less available for adults and their children to develop together.

Board Meetings fix this. They provide a form of experiential education—a type of learning that happens through engaging with people and the world, instead of through lectures.

It's the same kind of learning we discovered on the original surf trips that inspired us to create this movement. In the places we traveled to, and in the experiences we shared, we developed the life and character skills that helped us in our professional lives and personal relationships. We had no tests or certifications on those surf trips, but they helped us build businesses, learn valuable lessons, and improve our lives more than formal education ever could have.

Any expert in the field of education would tell you that lectures are less powerful than experience, yet as parents, our usual approach is to lecture kids at the kitchen table.

Think back to when you were a kid and ask yourself how effective it was for you, and how much affection you felt, as your parents and teachers lectured you. I suspect you'll remember what most parents do: that lectures didn't work for you.

They won't work for your kids, either.

Experiential education—what you're doing when you dedicate time for a focused and fun Board Meeting with your child— turns this around. Yes, it takes more planning, more effort, and more creativity; it is indeed harder than lecturing. But the rewards are undeniable. Board Meetings send your child the powerful message that they are loved and important, while teaching them the lessons that lecturing never could.

❧

GARY'S STORY

"As a frequently deploying Navy submarine commander, I had been away from my two sons for most of their life. My wife had been forced into single-parent status.

She was tired, and I carried a lot of guilt. The kids were growing distant and this all resulted in frequent arguments and sometimes shouting matches.

I was desperately trying to make up for lost time with my oldest son who was already in high school, and I was trying to bring warmth and trust back into our family. To begin that process, we dove into the deep end and attended a Family Board Meetings retreat.

My son was hesitant to go to the first event; he did not want speak in front of the group, any group, about his relationship and feelings. When we arrived, it got worse; a few attendees that had gone through recent tragedies were very emotional in the opening moments and he got nervous. I kept reinforcing that there were no requirements—that he did not have to share or join in. Jim and the other facilitators made the difference. They immediately connected with him as an equal. In the end, we couldn't STOP him from sharing. I was incredibly impressed and deeply grateful. That event and the Board Meeting Strategy saved our family.

Now, the arguments at home are almost non-existent. We have family dinner almost every evening. We openly discuss what happens at school, the temptations of drugs, cigarettes, alcohol, and many other subjects we'd never have discussed before. My son and I both have continued our daily gratitude journals.

There's been a massive increase in trust between my son and me, and we've adopted a number of family-first practices as a result of what we've learned. Including this Board Meeting Strategy every 90 days. Now, when anything happens or someone says something that is surprising in our house, our initial thought is that it was meant out of love. We trust that we want the best for each other, that we have each other's back.

It is hard to put into words the importance and impact that a personal connection has made for my son. There are very few concerns anymore that he wouldn't bring directly to his mother or me, but I really appreciate that Jim makes himself always available and that my son goes to him before some of the much worse choices he has at school."

☙

CONNECT WITH OUR COMMUNITY

Readers of *The Family Board Meeting* and parents that are already implementing the strategy have created a community of like-minded individuals from around the world to support each other in this journey. This is a strong online community in which to connect, support, share best practices, learn from one another and discuss the book. Check it out here: www.facebook.com/boardmeetingstribe

—6—

BOARD MEETINGS IN ACTION

I can't think of a better example to illustrate the power of the three steps than that of a Board Meeting I had years ago with my son Leland. It's a great example of how the three steps work and the connection and learning that followed.

As you know, the child must choose the activity, but I was a bit surprised when Leland chose to go to the St. Augustine lighthouse for our Board Meeting.

The lighthouse was built in the 1800s and is about 165 feet high. The only way to get to the top is by climbing more than 200 steps up a staircase that spirals through the building. Leland's brother had chosen the lighthouse for a Board Meeting not long before and was raving about the experience of getting to the top.

I suspected that was the reason Leland wanted to do it, but I was still surprised. Leland has a fear of heights, and normally, something like climbing a giant set of iron stairs to the top of a tower wouldn't even be something he'd consider.

Still, I thought it was a great idea, and I was interested to see how the experience would play out.

The Board Meeting started out as they all do. Leland and I got together for the ritual of turning off electronics. I said my famous (and predictable) line, "Is my phone going to be on today?"

"Nope," he answered with a smile.

After turning off the electronics, we said our good-byes to Jamie and Alden and hopped in my car. As we crossed the bridge into St. Augustine, I was becoming more curious as to whether or not Leland would make the climb—he was starting to look a bit nervous.

Leland's fear of heights is well known in our family, and Jamie even mentioned to me before the Board Meeting that she wasn't sure if he'd do it. We discussed it and agreed it was a great chance for him to give it a try. I certainly wasn't going to say to him, "You're scared of heights. Are you even going to climb the lighthouse when we get there?" Instead, Jamie and I agreed the best thing to do was to simply go along with the plan and see what he'd do.

Sure enough, his nervousness grew as we got closer, and when we pulled into the parking lot, he started freaking out. I simply reassured him that this Board Meeting was his choice and that I wasn't going to force him to do anything.

For all his anxiety, though, I sensed he wanted to overcome this obstacle. Why else would he have chosen the exact thing he's scared of? I considered our options. I knew the stairs to the top of the lighthouse were split with landings along the way that would make perfect resting places, so I gently suggested, "You chose to come here, Leland. You don't have to do anything, but what if we just went up to that first level? We don't have to go the whole way."

It took him a while to think it over, but eventually he agreed to walk up the stairs to the first landing. Once there, we sat down and took a break. Again, I gently suggested we could go up one more set of stairs or go back down. Again, he timidly (although a little less so) agreed to give it a try.

We continued this way, flight after flight, landing after landing. Finally, after few more periods of climbing and resting, we were close to the top. I said, "We're closer to the top than the bottom. Now that we're this close, do you want to just go all the way up before walking back down?" By then, he was feeling confident, and he agreed with more gusto than before.

Eventually, we reached the very top, where we were overtaken by the breathtaking view. Leland was thrilled with the beauty, but his thrill at the view was nothing compared to his pride at going all the way to the top. The Board Meeting was already a huge success, and we savored the moment for a while before heading back down.

To my surprise, the moment we got to the bottom, Leland wanted to climb it again. This was a different kid than the one who arrived at the lighthouse less than an hour before! He had no fear on the second climb, and we did the whole thing without stopping. We descended again, and sure enough, he wanted to go right back up!

Luckily for me (I was getting tired!), the lighthouse keepers had stopped climbing for the rest of the day due to the threat of lightning. I breathed a sigh of relief, and Leland mentioned that since we couldn't go up again, he was ready to go to his favorite café, where we had already agreed we'd go after the lighthouse.

As we always do on a Board Meeting, we shared a meal together, chatted, and enjoyed each other's company. We talked a lot, but this meal was not yet the focused reflection time—we have a ritual for that. After we eat, we often go to Leland's favorite beach where you can hear the waves as they crash. We'll climb onto the rocks, relax, and have a chat.

In the early days, the focused reflection would start with me asking him what part of the day was his favorite. Now that we're dialed into the process, however, I don't even have to ask him. He starts talking spontaneously.

On this day, the theme was apparent, and we moved gently into a conversation about overcoming fears. Leland asked me if I'd ever been scared. Imagine that for a moment; to our kids, we seem so bulletproof that they assume we don't feel fear.

Notice, I didn't force him into an awkward conversation. There was no lecture. It was a natural evolution—he had just finished overcoming a fear, and he wanted to know about my life experiences.

This was a perfect chance for real vulnerability. I thought about it for a moment, then told him about several times in the past when I was afraid. I also explained that fears are normal, that we will always have them, and that we can overcome them by taking small actions just like we did at the lighthouse.

What I didn't do was try to pack in a long lecture about all of the little ways I thought Leland could improve, nor did I drone on and on. The focused reflection took just a few minutes, and when he was ready, we walked back to the car and headed home. It was as simple as that.

I couldn't have scripted the Board Meeting any better if I'd tried. I could have told him a thousand times that he has to face his fears, but it wouldn't have had one-thousandth the effect the Board Meeting did. Experiential education won the day.

Leland was happy and energetic for days after his revelation about overcoming fear. And it wasn't just him, either. Jamie and I both beamed with pride when my friend asked him about his Board Meeting and he responded with a heartfelt (and elegant, I might add) talk about the importance of facing one's fears.

Once again, the simple Board Meetings strategy had a lasting impact on a young child and his family. Leland developed a stronger character that day, and I saw this brave boy in a whole new light. And, naturally, I was proud of the role I played in helping him overcome his fear.

Not every Board Meeting will have this obvious of a lesson—sometimes the lessons are more subtle, the connection more gradual. Don't expect visible, profound results, or put pressure on creating the perfect meeting. The process works even when it's not this picture perfect, and the relationship builds even when it doesn't play out as vividly as tackling a fear of heights.

Trust the process, enjoy the moment—you're doing the most important job in the world.

TOP TIPS FOR
A SUCCESSFUL
BOARD MEETING

The Board Meetings strategy is elegantly simple and tremendously effective, but even with three easy steps, the best intentions can sometimes go awry.

The last thing you want is for your Board Meeting to become just another thing your kid feels forced to endure. Here are the best ways to ensure your time together is just as amazing as you hope.

1. BE COMPLETELY PRESENT

No matter what, don't concern yourself with other matters during the Board Meeting. Anything else can wait a few hours. Just focus on what you are doing with your son or daughter.

This may sound simple, but it's not always easy in practice. Consider that the day of your Board Meeting might be the same day you lose a big contract. Perhaps it will be the day your father tells you he has cancer. Maybe it's the day you receive a phone call from your child's principal about bad behavior.

Even if none of these things happen, pressure and unexpected events are facts of life. If you wait for the perfect, stress-free moment before giving your child your full attention, you'll be waiting forever.

Seize the moment before you. Turn off the phone, make a real effort to turn off the voices in your mind, and simply focus on your child.

2. DROP YOUR GUARD

One of the most exciting findings in psychology over the past few years has been the power of vulnerability. Brené Brown's 2010 TED talk went viral and set the stage for the vulnerability revolution—and for good reason; wherever true vulnerability is practiced, relationships grow, strengthen, and become more rewarding.

It can be difficult, however, for parents to be open and vulnerable. We're trained to be tough, confident and strong for our children. But while those things can be important, there's great value in letting your guard down and revealing more of yourself to your child.

Keeping your guard up is far more common than we care to admit; you may not even realize you're doing it.

Now's the time to change that. Be aware of how you're feeling, open up, and enjoy authentic communication.

3. DON'T CRAM IN TOO MUCH CONTENT

I know we all have a long list of lectures lined up that we believe our kids need to hear, but those lectures are probably the surest path to losing both their trust *and* any interest in future Board Meetings.

Keep the focused reflection light (especially at the beginning). By spending quality time together, you've already spoken volumes without speaking a word.

Resist the temptation to think of your time together as a schooling opportunity. If you treat your Board Meeting with a "to-do list" mentality, you'll lose your kid the very first time. Board Meetings are about creating space; let that space grow. As trust is built, conversations will happen.

4. SAY WHAT YOU'RE HOLDING BACK

This is something you'll only understand once you're in a Board Meeting. At a certain point in your time together, once you've had fun, eaten a meal, and had some focused reflection, you'll end up reaching a moment of emotional clarity where you want to say something meaningful.

Say it.

If you hold back when that opportunity comes, you'll regret it. Vulnerability must be met with vulnerability— if your child trusts you enough to be vulnerable, you must reciprocate.

Have you ever confided in someone and then regretted it afterward? Have you ever opened your mouth and been met with a blank stare rather than empathy and reciprocal vulnerability? If this has happened to you, I'd wager that you stopped being open and vulnerable with that person from that moment on.

The same is true of our interactions with our kids. Have you ever heard a child or teenager say of their parents, "They just don't understand?" Of course you have—you've probably said it yourself. The feeling of being misunderstood by one's parents is widespread, and it's usually due to a vulnerability gap. The only way to let your kids know that you really *do* understand is to be vulnerable—and that means saying what you're holding back.

This can be surprisingly difficult, but *just do it*. It only takes a few moments of courage to say something meaningful that your child may remember for a lifetime. That authentic statement of love and appreciation you're thinking about, but hesitating to say, could be the game changer in taking your relationship to a new level.

5. YOU ABSOLUTELY MUST HAVE FUN

Our experience has taught us that fun is the secret sauce of all successful Board Meetings. Raising kids can seem like serious business, but the ability to have fun with your children is a crucial ingredient for creating connection.

If you can't let go and enjoy yourself with your kids, they'll notice. Even in an environment they enjoy, they'll pick up on your stiffness—they may even feel slighted by your inability to have fun with them, or assume that you'd just rather be somewhere else.

Sadly, many of us have simply forgotten how to have fun, or only know how to have fun in an "adult" way, like having drinks with our friends. One of the best things about having children is that they can remind us of just how freeing it is to be child-like. To let that happen, though, you need to relax, let go, and accept them as your teacher.

Many of us can't imagine letting ourselves be guided by a child because we're accustomed to our role of guiding them, but there is nobody more qualified to teach fun than a kid. Every single child is born with a Ph.D. in fun!

Let them be your teacher. They will love and respect you for letting go and playing with them, but don't do it for them. Do it for *you*. Do it because play feels good. It's vital to a successful Board Meeting, it's vital for your relationship, and it's vital for your *life,* so get into your fun zone the moment the Board Meeting starts.

You must, absolutely, have fun.

❧

At the heart of all these tips is a single idea: if you're going to hold Board Meetings, then give yourself over to them completely. Commit fully—not just in time, but in your focus and your emotional presence.

Board Meetings are simple and powerful. But if you're not prepared to execute them with consistency, love, and passion, they can become meaningless just like any other empty ritual.

—8—

FAQ'S

After many years, many parents, and many Board Meetings, we've heard a lot of questions. Here are answers to some of the best and most important.

HOW OLD DO KIDS NEED TO BE TO START HAVING BOARD MEETINGS?

We've found that the Board Meetings strategy can start being implemented as early as two and a half years old. During the first Board Meeting I had with my daughter Maggie, she fell asleep after three hours. Nonetheless, after that first one, she would often ask my wife, "When is my next meeting with Daddy?" I've gotten similar reports from others. Start 'em young when it comes to quality time!

There's also no upper age limit. Even if your kids have grown up and moved away, try for one Board Meeting a year. You're never too old for quality time.

HOW DO I GET STARTED? HOW DO I GET MY KIDS TO BUY IN? HOW DO I APPROACH THEM?

A common concern, especially with older children. First, let me tell you what *not* to do: don't go to your tween or teen and say, "I read a book on parenting and I want to try doing something with you that they taught me." Instant connection killer!

I'm all for honesty, but it's important to wrap an idea in a desirable package. No young person wants to feel like a lab rat for a parenting book strategy that, as far they know, might have some really annoying and embarrassing side effects.

What has worked for me is straight honesty without an agenda. Try these:

- "You're growing up fast, and I don't want to miss spending time with you."
- "I'd like to start having some set time together to hang out."

I also let the children miss school once in a while for a Board Meeting. Ask an adult whose parents have passed away if they would have been okay with their parents pulling them out of school occasionally to have that time together. What they usually say is, "Are you kidding me? Of course!"

ISN'T PLAYING HOOKY IRRESPONSIBLE?

I believe in a good education and the value of school. And I also believe in the value of hard work.

But I believe in the importance of our relationships more.

On occasion, we need to break the normal routine so that we can really remember what's most important. Work and school can easily dictate our schedule forever if we let them. I refuse to let this happen in my family. So, two to three days per year, each of my kids will miss school and I'll miss work to have a Board Meeting.

This makes perfect attendance loyalists and workaholics want to throw up. They are usually the first ones to say to me, "What kind of example are you setting?!"

This is something I've thought on a lot. I believe the example I'm setting is this:

When my kids grow up, they will have a habit instilled within them to play hooky from work and school every 90 days to spend time with their most important relationships—without remorse and without guilt. It will also prove to their own children that they can (and will) put their relationship ahead of their work.

Missing two days of school per year is a small price to pay for real connection between parent and child.

CAN YOU GIVE EXAMPLES OF SOME BOARD MEETING ACTIVITIES YOU OR OTHERS HAVE DONE WITH GREAT RESULTS?

Again, we want to let creation come from your son or daughter for buy-in and to avoid pushing our own "agenda," which happens more times than we like to admit. But here are a few guidelines.

Almost all Board Meetings include a meal of some sort—there's a simple connection to breaking bread together that's easy and natural. (Just like the activity of the day, I also let my sons or daughter choose the restaurant.)

Some Board Meeting activities we've had are:

Climbing the lighthouse, walking the beach, hiking, museums, cooking class, football games, baseball games, sporting events, live music, play or performance, horseback riding, go cart racing, pedicure/manicure, roller blading, biking, Pokémon class, at-home fashion show, trampoline world, rock climbing, shopping, water parks, boating, helicopter rides, zoo/animal preserve, basketball, yoga class, ice skating, golf/driving range, miniature golf, art class, photography class, robotics class, comedy show, ghost tours, planetarium, Segway tour, fishing, story hour, playing in the park, and laser tag.

Honestly, if you walked the same hike every time and then had a meal together, I believe the potency would still be there. Always remember that it's the quality time that matters most.

CAN YOU TELL ME MORE ABOUT THE "FOCUSED REFLECTION"? HOW CAN I GET STARTED?

For some, this piece feels uncomfortable, but it's important. It's what ties it all together and gets you below the surface. If it makes you uneasy, don't worry. The objective is simply to provide the encouragement and space to talk. It's not complicated.

Here are a few ideas to kick it off:

Give a genuine compliment.

"You were laughing so hard when you beat me in go-cart racing today. It reminded me to laugh more. Thank you."

"You were so persistent today when we were learning to ski. I'm proud of you."

Offer a sincere apology.

Is there anything you (the parent) would like to acknowledge and apologize for? "I know I brushed you off the other day when you were talking to me. I'm sorry about that."

Share a story of the past.

Discuss your strengths and weakness, things you struggled with.

"When I was your age…"

Use the simplest question of all.

"What was your favorite part of today?"

You can follow it with, "Why?"

I cannot express enough how this is *not* a time for you to discuss what more you need from your child, or to lecture on grades or chores. This is a time to focus on getting deeper.

WHAT ARE COMMON PITFALLS?

The most common pitfall is also the most easily remedied: not scheduling your Board Meetings. When I first started working with some highly successful and busy people, I found that 80 percent of the time, failure came from simply not scheduling the meeting in advance.

These were busy mothers and fathers working at a high level—most of their lives were run by their calendars. All they had to do to solve the problem was simply *schedule* it—either themselves, or have their staff do it. Yet they skipped that step, and it cost them.

Just do it. Now. It takes only seconds, and it almost guarantees success.

Another pitfall is not letting your child choose the activity. This can easily lead to them being disengaged or "bored" with what the parent picked. Let go, and let your child choose. If you simply show genuine enthusiasm and a willingness to go all-in and follow your child's lead, you'll make some game-changing deposits to your relationship, instead of painful withdrawals.

Lastly, this is not a time to discipline or lecture on all the improvements *they* need to make. Although feel free to share improvements that you yourself might need to work on. :)

DOES THIS STRATEGY WORK WITH OTHER RELATIONSHIPS BESIDES WITH CHILDREN? DO YOU DO THESE WITH YOUR SPOUSE?

Yes! Quality time is the common thread of all close human connection; the principles of this strategy work in strengthening any relationship. Grandparent-grand-child, aunt-nephew, Big Brother volunteer-Little Brother sponsor, friend-friend, sibling-sibling, and yes, even between spouses.

Board Meetings are about connection, so they can work with anyone you value in your life. Best of all, you have almost nothing to lose! For just a few hours of time, you open the possibility to transform your most important relationships and simplify your home life for the better.

WON'T BEING ONE-ON-ONE WITH MY CHILD TAKE AWAY FROM THE FAMILY DYNAMIC?

Absolutely not, and the best way to describe why is to share a childhood memory. I remember watching the New York Giants' summer football camp as a child and seeing the team break up into small practice groups. After having their separate practices, they came back together to practice as a whole team.

These individual practice sessions help the team improve by first separating and strengthening the individual parts, so they can come together as a stronger whole. The same thing happens when you spend one-on-one time with each of your children: individual relationships grow stronger, and they connect and strengthen the whole family.

One-on-one time is crucial for a couple of reasons. First, we know that children start developing individuality around the age of nine. At that age, their self-concept becomes very important, and as parents, we need to recognize each child as a unique person. Nothing works better to achieve this than one-on-one time. It shows our kids that we honor their individuality.

Second, children often don't want to discuss certain issues in a group setting. Only one-on-one time maximizes trust and intimacy enough to make a child feel comfortable enough to speak about anything. I come from a family of five children, and I remember not wanting to talk about certain things in front of my siblings. By creating a special one-on-one space, we encourage real openness between parent and child.

ANY OTHER SUGGESTION TO MAKE THE MOST OF OUT THIS STRATEGY?

One thing I noticed after a year or two of using this strategy was that the events start to run together. I realized I might be losing touch with some of the most powerful moments of my life.

Now, I take a photo at each Board Meeting, and then jot down a few moments of the time together. When was it? What did we do? What were our top reflections and highlights?

My goal is that when my kids leave the house, I can hand them a simple reflection journal of our times together that they will always cherish.

EIGHTEEN SUMMERS

A mentor once told me: *you only get eighteen summers with your kids, so make the most of them.*

It's easy to think you get more—after all, most of us get *decades* with our kids. Don't we?

Not exactly. If you do the math—and I'm going to warn you right now that the math is frightening—by the time your kids finish high school, you've probably spent *most* of the time with them that you're going to. That's right: by the time your kids leave home, in terms of the number of hours, *you've already spent the vast majority of the time with them that you ever will.*

Don't believe me? Think about it. Before they become adults—during those "eighteen summers"—you're with your kids a *lot*. Almost full-time for those first years, but then still fairly intensely after that.

But how often will you see them when they move out and have lives of their own? Holidays? The odd visit?

The point my mentor was trying to make is that that time is short. *Carpe diem*. Before you know it, those eighteen summers are gone. Grab 'em while you can.

But the lesson of quality time teaches us another lesson. It teaches us that the *quantity* of time, while important, is a pale imitation of *quality*. Quality time is the elixir of connection. It's potent stuff. And the best part of something so potent is that you don't need much of it to get a great result.

A few years ago, I donated a kidney to my father. One of the most critical ingredients of that process was my reconnection to him. Our eighteen summers had long since passed us by. We were both grown men. I had kids of my own, and we were going through our own summers together as a family.

But Board Meetings had taught me a lot about quality time. And so, my father and I began our own variation on the Board Meetings strategy. Decades after I was child, my father and I began spending quality time together.

It worked. Despite our ages and all the years that had passed, it worked. After so many, many years, I discovered that deep connection is a possibility at any age, between anyone.

It was then that I realized that you *can* have more than eighteen summers. I saw that quality time creates a kind of loophole in the equation— a way to get *more* out of time, no matter how little of it you may have together.

Too little time is a common challenge for all of us. In those moments when you feel you don't have enough, ask yourself this:

Do you really need more time in order to connect with the people around you, or do you just need *better* time?

TAKING ACTION

The lesson of this book is that time and quality time are not the same thing. I hope it's abundantly clear by now that quality time is infinitely more valuable. And that means one magical thing: *no matter where you are in your life, you can create quality time with your kids.*

In seven years, I have never missed a Board Meeting with my children. Making it a priority not only strengthened our family but gave me an anchor during some of the stormiest moments in business and life. My goal in writing this book is to give you the tools and the knowledge to do the same thing.

We've discussed real-life examples of how the Board Meetings strategy works. We've examined why it's so effective, and we've looked at each of the steps in detail. I hope by now you feel a sense of urgency about connecting with your child. I hope you're ready to take action.

Still, I know some readers won't do it, despite the simplicity and all the benefits. This makes me sad because

I know what it can do for every parent and their child. I've experienced it myself.

Here's what I suggest: right now, at this very moment (yes, *now*), stop and take a look at your schedule. Now take a look at your child's schedule. Find a day that works for both and schedule a Board Meeting.

Do it now.

Just like that, the biggest hurdle to reconnection will be behind you. It's that simple.

Schedule it, and then re-read this book a day or two before your Board Meeting. Re-reading will ensure you remember how to execute every step. Then, when the day comes, you'll only have one job: to simply enjoy it.

We would love to hear from you after your first Board Meeting. Please feel free to contact us at info@ boardmeetings.com to tell us your story and get helpful feedback if you need it.

Thank you for your care and attention.

Sincerely,
Jim Sheils

THE POWER OF BOARD MEETINGS

Real Stories from Real Families

DAN MARTELL'S STORY

I started doing board meetings three years ago when the kids were super young—they are four and five now. I read the book on a Saturday morning, and the next day I scheduled the first board meeting. I said to my wife, "For the rest of my life, I want to do this with our boys."

I was trying to add a higher level of quality one-on-one time. Because there are two of them, and they're so close in age, they play together a lot. I wanted more individual time.

That was something I never had with my dad. I love my dad, and feel lucky to have him. He's my hero. But to this day, I can't remember a time when my dad and I hung out one-on-one, overnight. Ever. I can't imagine how our relationship would be different if we had.

I started with Max initially, because Noah really couldn't even talk to tell me what he wanted to do. They're old enough now that they're starting to talk about the next meeting. They say things like, "Hey! Next board meeting, we're going to go surfing." Or, "The next meeting we're going bowling."

The boys love it. They tease each other about it, saying things like, "Oh we did something. I can't tell you. It's a secret." They get very excited about it.

I'm playing the long game with these board meetings. What I'm most excited about is that one moment—it could be in one year, it could be ten—where we've created a space for them to share something that might otherwise have gone unsaid. I know that in my life those moments just never came up because there was no place to do it.

Out of all the stuff I do, if I had to pick one thing, one ritual, one rhythm that I do with all my kids, this is the one. This is the most important thing I do with them.

❦

DAVID BACH'S STORY

When I first tried a Board Meeting, I was already super-close with my son, Jack, who was 13 at the time.

I had heard about Family Board Meetings a number of times from groups like Strategic Coach and Genius Network. I loved the concept—something that takes into account the perspective of an entrepreneur AND focuses on family. But, I always found a reason—too much work, too much travel—to not try it.

Our very first Board Meeting experience exceeded anything I could have hoped for in my wildest imagination. In just a few short hours, Jack and I bonded like we've never bonded before. I felt even closer to him. I got to hear what his dreams are and I now get to support him in those dreams. That is something that never would have happened without following the Board Meeting strategy.

I also am grateful to have spent time with him in an intentional way—it was unlike a vacation or simple father-son time. I came away from the experience with unbelievable gratitude for the relationship I have with my son. After our first Board Meeting, Jack looked at me and asked, "Dad, when can we do this again?" I even asked him if he would rather do a Board Meeting or go on vacation. His response: Board Meeting. This time together was truly a gift.

℧

BRAD JOHNSON'S STORY

I was first exposed to Jim's family board meeting framework when I attended a dad's retreat out in Philadelphia, Pennsylvania where Jim spoke. It in-

stantly made sense to me as it seemed like a simple rhythm I could implement to deepen my relationship with each of my children. At the time, my boys were four and five.

The biggest thing for me to make it happen was getting it on the calendar. From there, it was really just turning the phone on airplane mode and being fully present.

Typically, we do Board Meetings on Saturdays or Sundays, and after the activity of their choosing, we do lunch at the same pizza parlour. It's really become a family ritual and I've just found the openness and the questions that follow them are on a whole other level after being so fully present. In my experience, do it one time, and it will be a family ritual forever.

❧

JAYSON GAIGNARD'S STORY

My daughter was really young when I started (3 years old). If anything, the benefit initially was more for me as I had a hard time establishing a connection with my daughter for the first few years of her life. Now, the benefit of Family Board Meetings are mutual, and we both eagerly anticipate them. My daughter looks forward to them months in advance. I also now do quarterly board meetings with my wife, which has been HUGE.

BOOK *THE FAMILY BOARD MEETING*
BEST-SELLING AUTHOR
JIM SHEILS TO SPEAK

Book Jim as your keynote speaker and your audience will see near-instant remarkable results in connecting deeper with their children and spouses—even in the workplace.

Jim promises that your audience will leave compelled to connect more deeply with their children, spouses, and co-workers. He offers them a framework for relationships, enhanced by plans and tools that make improvement in the relationships fast, effective, and sustainable. In fact, many audience members take the first steps toward positive action before even leaving the event! Available for hour-long keynote presentations, workshop-style talks, or private event trainings, Jim Sheils is sure to inspire, challenge and set in motion your audience and team.

Topics include:

- 18 Summers: How to Make the Most of the Time You've Got

- The Family Board Meeting: Reconnect and Deepen The Relationship with Your Child

- Pizza Friday: Using Service and Contribution to Teach Our Children Confidence & Purpose

- The Education Matrix: How to Ensure Your Kids are Getting the Important Lessons Not Taught in School

For more information, visit www.18summers.com

CONNECT ONLINE

Readers of *The Family Board Meeting* and along with those already implementing the strategy, have created a community of like-minded parents from around the world to support each other in this journey. This is a strong online community in which to connect, support, share best practices, learn from one another and discuss the book. Check it out here: www.facebook.com/boardmeetingstribe.

Follow us on YouTube:

https://www.youtube.com/channel/UC06q57ph-1irsY2hGGw6dOQ?view_as=subscriber

and Instagram:

https://www.instagram.com/18summerstribe/ to share your #18summers stories with us.

VOLUME DISCOUNTS

Share *The Family Board Meeting* with your employees, co-workers, Book Club, church organization or any large group by reaching out to info@boardmeetings.com.

ABOUT THE AUTHOR

Motivated by what he saw as one of the most tragic challenges of modern life—the disconnection of busy entrepreneurs from their families—Jim developed the Family Board Meeting process to help business owners bridge the gaps between themselves and their loved ones.

Since then, both Jim's message and his book, the best-selling *The Family Board Meeting,* have spread around the globe. Often called "Crazy Glue" for families, Jim's popular and simple frameworks now reach thousands of parents worldwide, helping them feel more connected with their kids, be happier at home and leave a lasting legacy.

Jim is the founder of Family Board Meetings, which specializes in live events, workshops and private consulting for organizations and parents looking to strengthen their family life while still succeeding in business. He's an in-demand public speaker, and owns a private real estate company that has done over $200 million in transactions.

Jim is an avid surfer and enjoys traveling with family and friends, especially his beautiful wife Jamie and their four children, Alden, Leland, Magnolia, and Sampson. His greatest adventure to date? Donating a kidney to the best guy on the planet, his father.